God has graced Alisha Broughton with great insight and wisdom. As her spiritual father, I have seen her grow into a highly motivated and articulates woman of God. It's a pleasure seeing her in print. Readers of her writing will be enlightened and helped by her years of experience.

A Proud Spiritual Father

Apostle Ivory L. Hopkins

Founder and Overseer of Pilgrims

Ministry of Deliverance

Living on the Edge

Poetic Verse

By: Alisha L. Broughton

Living on the Edge

By: Alisha L. Broughton - Poetic Verse

Cover design by: Anelda L. Ballard

Cover Photograph by: Nova Development Corporation

Logo designs by: Andre M. Saunders

Editor: Alisha L. Broughton

Assistant Editor: Anelda L. Ballard

Photographs by: www.photobucket.com and www.inmagine.com

© 2009 Alisha L. Broughton

ISBN 978-0-9843255-0-4

ISBN 0-9843255-0-6

Library of Congress Control Number: 2009944151

All rights reserved. This book is protected under the copyright laws of the United States of America. This book may not be copied or reprinted for commercial gain or profit. The use of short quotations or occasional page copying for personal or group study is permitted and encouraged. Permission will be granted upon request.

For Worldwide Distribution. Printed in the United States of America

Published by Jazzy Kitty Greetings Marketing & Publishing, LLC

Utilizing Microsoft Publishing Software

ACKNOWLEDGMENTS

Without God, I am nothing. God, I thank you for all of my wealth and success this is about to come. God, you are the one that deserves the praise. I give special thanks to my mother, Beverly Broughton-Singletary, without her I would never have been born. Next, thank you dads, Vaun-Dyke Ford and Asst. Pastor Benjamin Singletary. Thanks to my wonderful, intellectual divas my daughters Ashley and Amber Broughton. They pushed me to publish and become a motivational speaker. You two are the baddest divas that I have ever seen. You will go places in life because God said so and it was inherited by your mother, me.

Grandmother, I love you. Boy, we have come along way together. I pray that God continues to sustain your health without you what would I do. A very special dedication to a special friend that passed away before my book was completed, Army Specialist Mark Anthony Piper. Boy, I miss you so much. I think about each day how you called me and told me I was living beneath my privileges and get my act together. Many days I was upset with you but we had a special friendship. We both told each other like it was. I miss all of your jokes! You were there for me when others gave up. I will miss you!

Thanks to my cousins Lakeia, Vaun-Tae, Waneka, Jeanetta, Valiere, Kungkeya, for telling me time and time again to keep my head high. We have had rough times in our family but today you will celebrate with me. To all my nieces and nephews, Auntie loves you, Jordan, Bonica, Tytona, Benjore, Kema, Shawneise, Aunyae, Anijia, L.B., Kymora and Bryant. When I make money, I will pay for your college tuition. You guys keep me busy and make me read to you when I am tired. I love you Aunt Annie Mae! You are a woman full of inspiration and encouragement. To my special friends and there are not that many, Melodie Thomas-Price, Lisa Lindsay Scott,

Sarah Mullen, Rosemary Brown, Anelda Ballard, Nannette Mann, Linda Lewis, Angela Ayres, and Leanna Waples. Thanks for being in my life. I have different relationships with you all! Thanks for providing me with a shoulder to cry on. My grandparents, Frank and Bell Singletary, and Catherine Sermon.

Thanks to my Aunt Darlene and her husband Greg. My uncle Tyrone, follow in my steps. All of my neighborhoods some good, some bad but you all made me at Park Royal. Special thanks to Martha Piper for your encouragement. To my mentors in the gospel, Apostle Hopkins, Overseer at Pilgrims Ministry of Deliverance, you are the man. You have been my Overseer for 18 years. Thanks for believing in me and giving me hope. Words can not express my gratitude. I appreciate you and First Lady Evelyn Hopkins. Bishop Levin Bailey and First Lady Rose Bailey, Pilgrims Ministry, thank you for your hospitality and love.

Thank you Pastor David Shockley and First Lady Shirl (Myrna) Shockley of Jesus Love Temple, Milford, DE. Pastor Brangman and First Lady Brangman of Mt. Zion on Georgetown/Lewes Highway. You have been there for me. Bishop Roland Mifflin and Co-Pastor Lynn Mifflin, Power and Love Ministries of Dagsboro, DE. Bishop Roy Bryant and Mother Bryant of the Bible Church of Christ, I grew up here and think of you frequently. Bishop Ed Cannon and wife Jocelyn Cannon, BCC, miss you and thank you. Elder Emma Sample-Thomas, BCC, you are an awesome woman of God.

Pastor Debra Rider, you are an awesome woman of God in the Gospel. Thanks a bunch! You're like a mother to me. Welton Evans of Evans Trucking thanks for your words of encouragement. I appreciate all of my mentors in the ministry.

DEDICATION

This book is dedicated to Specialist Mark Anthony Piper

DEDICATION

God, called you home
At such an early age
I will miss you forever
And everyday

Why did you leave us?
Only God knows why
You will always have a place
In my heart
And that's a start

A start for God to take the pain away
You will always be missed
And I will continue to pray
For your family each time.

You were a trooper
A true friend indeed
Words cannot express my gratitude
Of what you meant to me

I think about you daily
And the tears continue to flow

(Continued)

DEDICATION

I continue to pray

But only God knows

This is not a good-bye

Because you accepted Christ

He changed your life

In the wink of an eye

The day you passed away you sent

Me a text

You said,

"I appreciate you

Thanks for being that special friend."

You are a dynamite and an exceptional friend.

As I WRITE this book,

I say to you,

You are not forgotten

And this is true.

You are missed!

TABLE OF CONTENTS

Introduction…………………………………………………	i
Helping Hands……………………………………………..	01
A Path to Righteous………………………………………..	03
Broken Hearts……………………………………………...	05
Hurting and Loving……………………………………….	08
Inspire……………………………………………………...	10
God I Love You…………………………………………...	12
Hope………………………………………………………..	14
Who Are You?…………………………………………….	16
Understanding Change……………………………………	18
Why Did God Take You?………………………………..	20
If Loving You Is Wrong…………………………………..	22
The Joy I Feel…………………………………………….	24
Christ Vs. The Enemy (Devil) ………………………….	26
You are Appreciated…………………………………….	28
The Cares of the Life……………………………………	30
Your Return………………………………………………..	32
Breakthrough………………………………………………	35
Don't Take Control of My Mind…………………………	38
Understand Who You Are……………………………….	40
If All Eyes Could See……………………………………	42
Keeping It Real……………………………………………	45
The Earth Has Purpose…………………………………..	48

TABLE OF CONTENTS

When the Way has been Made.. 50

Forgiving... 52

Sharing the Dream... 54

Loving You is Easy... 56

Lord, I Thank You.. 58

Understanding Life 60

About the Author... 62

Letters... 64

Picture of Me and My Family.. 68

INTRODUCTON

My life has been rough. There have been many up's and down's but I made it. I bring you greetings and introduce you to my book entitled, Living on the Edge. This is a book of poetic verses to encourage you and uplift your spirits. I think about Apostle Ivory Hopkins, Pilgrims Ministry of Deliverance, his mini-sermons, "On a Spiritual Place Called Next." Regardless of my weaknesses, in character. I am still an anointed, appointed Woman of God. To God be all the Glory!

During the most revolutionary time in our lives, all we can do is trust God. We must hold onto a positive vision. What has God instilled in you? What is your purpose in life to the world and in the ministry? The enemy does not foster our future or our eternity. It's our own fears that blind us to the truth and fear that holds us in bondage. Fear keeps us in a place of what we do not want instead of what we can have. We, as people of God, should have a harmonious, healthful way of living. With God's faith we never stand alone.

When the doctor's told me in 2005 that I would lose my vision within a year, I had begun to praise God for my healing. Yes, there were days where I felt like giving up. The Enemy spoke to my mind. Then there was one thing after another diabetics, thyroids, high cholesterol, memory lose, irritable bowel syndrome, cyst on my left breast, Fibromyalgia and the latest possible diagnosis that I am being tested for lupus. While taking over 11 pills a day... I read scriptures of healing and examined myself. God let me know that I went though all of that to be a testimony to someone else. It's not all about me but about God using me to do His will.

When I said, "No." God said, "YES." There are many ways that the

INTRODUCTION

Holy Spirit speaks to us to tell us to make a change. How many of us take heed? Look in the mirror today and examine-YOURSELF! At times our face nearly hits the ground before we will listen to His call. Faith gives me the inner security to strive to leave a legacy of hope. When I leave this world, I want to make a difference in someone else's life. We must keep our vision and expectations high! We focus on whatever we believe in. When we direct our minds we direct our lives. I want to leave you with this scripture.

Hebrews 10:35-38 35) So do not throw away your confidence; it will be richly rewarded. 36) You need to persevere so that when you have done the will of God, you will receive what he has promised. 37) For in just a very little while, "He who is coming will come and will not delay. 38) But my righteous one will live by faith. And if he shrinks back, I will not be pleased with him." 39) But we are not of those who shrink back and are destroyed, but of those who believe and are saved.

Jeremiah 29:11-11) For I know the thoughts that I think toward you, saith the LORD, thoughts of peace, and not of evil, to give you an expected end.

Proverbs 23:18-18) There is surely a future hope for you, and your hope will not be cut off.

Proverbs 24:14-14) Know also that wisdom is sweet to your soul; if you find it, there is a future hope for you, and your hope will not be cut off.

Blessings, Alisha Broughton, Author

HELPING HANDS

God saw me in my weakest hour.

God saw me and loved me with his divine power.

God said, "My child hold my hand."

There is purpose in your plan.

As a child I knew you would strive for the best.

I placed the power in you to hold others hands.

All that is in you is what you are.

You have the key to make the jump-start.

You encourage others and learned to love.

(Continued)

HELPING HANDS

You inspire others to show strength to grow.

Your kind words and tender heart

Has kept others from falling a part.

Words are divine.

Can't you see!!

I place the power in you to set others free.

Do you know the strength you have within.

You should look in the mirror

And want to win.

The devil's tactics are just a minor plan.

He wants to take you out.

God said, "NO, I have a better plan!

A plan to lend others a helping hand.

"Dedicated to Ms. Nancy Russell"

A PATH TO RIGHTEOUS

As you look both ways,

There is no one you know.

You question God where you should go.

Lord, if you are there

Answer my plea.

Lord, I am walking this path.

Please, set me free.

I am walking alone.

(Continued)

A PATH TO RIGHTEOUS

Where should I be?
No family, friends or church members
On this walk.

I feel so alone…
Lord, where do I start?

I took this journey before
And now here I am again…
I traveled this road before
God want is your plan.

As I begin to walk
I begin to pray
Lord, thank you God for showing me the way.

In the midst of every trial
There is a purpose to
Lord, thank you for empowering me
To see me through.

BROKEN HEARTS

At times my heart has been broken
And no one understood why
My heart has been broken
Because the enemy lied

My heart has been broken
Through my family
And friends as well

My heart has been broken
In the Church
And I wore a mask of shame
No one understood my purpose
And I felt I was the one to blame

When my heart was broken
I felt I never live again
When my heart was broken
I thought God
Where are u
In this mess

(Continued)

BROKEN HEARTS

Which is causing me

Deep stress

My heart has been broken

So many times

Before..

My heart has been broken

And I walked right out the door.

My heart had been broken

When I lived in sin

When I thought others were praying

They were not my true friends

They judged me

They scorned me

And they told me I lied

But little did they know

That God helped me to way the hurt

Good bye

Now when you see me

You can't look me in my eye

(Continued)

BROKEN HEARTS

Because you talked about me
And God convicted you by and by

You do not believe
In me
And never knew who I was
You just criticized me
And how God is saying
My daughter
You will make it
By and by.

HURTING AND LOVING

Trusting can be difficult to do.
Everyone must trust someone to see you through.

When you're hurt
It seems there is no end.
When your heart is broken
You wonder if God
Can ever provide you with a friend.

My heart seems to compass
My life is a mess.
How can this be?
When my spirit man should be free.

My heart feels like it's ripped a part.
I cry, "God tell me why?"
Why is there so much pain?
I feel inside.

I walk around and continue to smile.
The hurt is unbearable.
Lord, show me why.

(Continued)

HURTING AND LOVING

Lord, tell me what to do today.

Because this pain tears me away.

Who are true in the house of God?

Who do I trust?

To make a fresh start.

Learn to love.

Learn to forgive.

Learn to trust the people

So you can learn to live.

Hurting is a thing of the past.

Loving is what makes God's people last.

"Dedicated to Paula Hudson"
Exceptional Friend

INSPIRE

Inspire my dreams
Oh, Lord.

Inspire my heart
Oh, Lord.

Inspire those that I come in
Contact with
Oh, Lord.

Inspire my destiny
Oh, Lord.

Inspire my family and friends
Oh, Lord.

Inspire my spiritual life
Oh, Lord.

Inspire my place of work.

(Continued)

INSPIRE

Oh, Lord.

Inspire my church family

Oh, Lord.

Inspire my vision.

Oh, Lord.

Inspire my will to live according to your Word.

Oh, Lord.

Inspire me to forgive.

Oh, Lord.

Inspire me to Love

Oh, Lord.

In all these things.

Inspire me to go forth

Oh, Lord…

To complete your purpose.

And will in my life.

Inspire…Inspire…Inspire…

"Dedicated to Ms. Carol Reid"

GOD I LOVE YOU

God, I love you

More each day

God, I love you

Because You showed me the way

God, I love you

Because of who you are

God, I love you

Because you

Are a Blessing in the Storm

God, I love you

Because you keep

Me insane

God, I love you

Because you are never ashamed

God I love you

You took Ezekiel

(Continued)

GOD I LOVE YOU

Up in the Wheel

God, I love you
For providing me with meals

God, I love you
Because you are strong
And Mighty

God I love you
Alpha and Omega
The Beginning and the End

God I love you
Because you are my best friend

God I love you in the midst
Of it all
You kept me
Safe from all harm

God, I love you

HOPE

You let me see

Hope is what I have.

Hope is what I feel.

Hope is your faith

To be healed.

Hope is what keeps us going

Day by Day.

Hope each day is what sustains us

To Love and just pray.

Hope is Faith.

Faith is Hope.

Hope is what we believe in.

When our emotions tell us

We will not succeed

(Continued)

HOPE

Where is your hope?

It's planted in Christ.

Hope is joy.

Hope takes away the pain.

Hope enables us to lead the way.

Hope is victory,

In the midst of our storm.

Hope gives us a mission

When things persist to go wrong.

Hope grows each and everyday

Hope is like a flower

Sprouting to save the day.

Keep hoping

Hope is God's way.

WHO ARE YOU?

Who are you to judge me?

When you are such a mess
Who are you to judge me
When God said, "I am blessed!"

Who are you to judge me
When I live for who I am
Who are you to judge me
When God is my friend

Who are you to judge
For when I am living for Christ
Who are you to judge me
When I am loving God
And He is precise

No more games for me
The truth lies here today
When are you to judge me
When God leads the way

(Continued)

WHO ARE YOU?

Who are you to judge me
When I needed you the most
Who are you to judge me
When I looked up to you
The most

Who are you to judge me
When you never even knew me
Who are you to judge me
When Christ has set me free

Who are you to judge me
When I am born again
Who are you to judge me
When you are fill of sin within

Let's stop judging
So that we can be set free

Free in our hearts and minds
So Christ can set us here.

UNDERSTANDING CHANGE

As days go by

Life continues to change…

Change is the storm….

Change in the rain…

Change enables you to know

Who you are….

Where you have been

And where you are going…

Change means accepting

Things as though they were…

Change means acceptance

Dealing with the profound issues

At hand

Finding your heart and evaluating

Who you really are…

Understanding that life is not only about you…

(Continued)

UNDERSTANDING CHANGE

Change brings new adventures
New life…
New Hope…
Hopes to be healed…
Hopes to come out of poverty…

Change in the economy…
Change of mind…
Learning to change issues
And not accepting things as they are…

Changing your attitude,

Changing your heart...
Changing your spiritual being
To live without falling apart…

As change takes place...
It perfects...

And makes you who you are...
Changes let us accept our destiny
Why don't you change?

WHY DID GOD TAKE YOU?

What a wonderful friend you were?

But God saw to take you home

I asked God why?

Why did He leave me alone...

Was it your time to go?

Why did you leave?

It hurt me

To see you go

But now your free...

You were a jewel in my life

You encouraged me to the end.

You were a great Man of God

And you were a special friend.

Though you left me in body

I feel your Spirit each day

I continue to pray

That God take my pain away...

(Continued)

WHY DID GOD TAKE YOU?

When you left me

I felt empty inside

I cried and cried

And said God why did you take him

Without even a sign...

The last time I saw you

You joked with glee

And that let me know

That you wanted your heart to be free...

No more pains in life

No more bills to pay

You can now rest in God's arms

I know that I will see you someday…

YOU WILL BE MISSED!

"Dedicated to Mark Anthony Piper"

IF LOVING YOU IS WRONG…

Love you from the depths of my soul.
I love you for caring for me when I grow old…
I love you for who you are and who you can be…
I love you because you allow me to be free…

I love you when you are wrong…
I love you when you sing my song….
I love you for taking time with me
And telling me that you believe in me.

I love you for all that you do…
I love you when you pray me through…
I love you for your special ways…
I love you each and every day..

(Continued)

IF LOVING YOU IS WRONG…

I love you for being you..

I love you for seeing me through…

I love you when your up or down.

I love you when it takes time

For you to come around….

Loving through it all…

Sickness…

Pain….

Loss of Job…

Tragedy…

It all has no end…

But yet I am still able to love you through it all.

Love is tireless...

I love you for who you are…

"Dedicated to Carol Reid, October 2009"

Classmate

THE JOY I FEEL

The Joy I feel

Grows real each day

The Joy I feel

Makes me love

The evil away

The Joy I feel

Helps me to forgive

The Joy I feel

Gives me peace

From within

The Joy I feel

No one can understand

The Joy I feel

Because God delivered me

From the hands

Of Satan

(Continued)

THE JOY I FEEL

The Joy I feel

Helps me keep my Hope

When the enemy comes

I can defeat Him

And stand on my Slope

The Word of God

The Word

Gives me Joy

The Word

Gives me Hope

God I praise you

For Life

And Joy

To the Uttermost

CHRIST VS. THE ENEMY (DEVIL)

The enemy wants you to believe
That you are not loved.
The enemy wants you to believe
There's no God above.

The enemy whispers in your ear.
The enemy lies to you so
You no longer care.
The enemy sends people
To self-destruct your name.
Because the enemy wants you to live
In embarrassment and a shame.

(Continued)

CHRIST VS. THE ENEMY (DEVIL)

The enemy will tell you that you are no good.

The enemy will have you be misunderstood.

The enemy comes to seek who he can devour.

The enemy knows that he is a liar.

The enemy wants you to be alone.

The enemy wants you to remain at home.

The enemy wants you to be desolate

With no friends.

His game plan is to make you

Feel there is no end.

The enemy is strong

But God will reign

So, the next time the enemy comes

And says, "You are no good

And should live in shame.

Tell the devil

He is a liar

Because Jesus Christ is the Savior

And the Word of God proves that the devil is a liar.

YOU ARE APPRECIATED

When was the last time

I told you I appreciated you

When was the last time

That you had a clue

You are dynamite

And fearfully made

You are a jewel

In your own special way

You are one of a kind

And you are a friend

You are true and will love the Lord until the end.

You are appreciated

When you speak into my life.

You are appreciated

Because you made a difference in my life.

You are appreciated just because of who you are.

You are appreciated and loved me

From the start

(Continued)

YOU ARE APPRECIATED

You never judged me
And you were always there
You loved the hell right out of me
And then you still cared

You appreciated me
When I was wrong
And you appreciated me when I was right.

You appreciated me
In my darkest hour
You continued to pray
That I would one day live right

You appreciated me even when I refused
To walk in my gift
You appreciated me and loved me
And I know this

You are appreciated just for who you are
I love you
Because you believed in me
And you gave me a start

THE CARES OF THIS LIFE

The cares of this life

Can get you down,

The cares of this life.

Will leave you with a frown.

God is our hope

To eternal life

God will take all the cares away

And turn your dark into day

The cares of this life

Can cause you pain.

The cares of this life

(Continued)

THE CARES OF THIS LIFE

Will allow you to see only bitterness

And rain.

The cares of this life

Are so detrimental indeed

That they make you lose focus

And you are no longer free.

The cares of this life

Should not get you down.

Remember Jesus will turn

Your whole life around.

The next time your in a storm.

The devil can do you no harm.

Because God holds your hands

And he is the King with the ultimate

Plan…

YOUR RETURN

We played around

Day-to-Day

Not even knowing

If you would come back some day

We took you for granted

And forgot that you were Lord

We laughed, we cried

And still did not recognize that you were Lord.

We heard who you were

But still lived a life of sin

We refused to accept you

And now it's the end.

(Continued)

YOUR RETURN

The angels blew their horn
As I looked around
Where have my friends gone?
No where to be found.

The saints witnessed to me
And I refused to listen
I thought they were crazy
And should be placed in prison

I thought my friends
Had lost their minds
Talking about a man named Christ
I thought they had lost it
And they invented Jesus Christ…

Now, that the rapture has come back
I am left behind
I do not want to go to hell
I had heard about it so many times…

(Continued)

YOUR RETURN

The place called hell

Frightened my heart

And now it's too late

I wish I listened from the start…

I missed the rapture

Now, I have no fate

I am begging God

God, please have mercy

Even though, I know it's to late…

Don't miss the rapture

Dedicated to Paula Hudson

And the Delaware Breast Cancer Coalition

BREAKTHROUGH

God, I ask for a breakthrough today
Why is there so much pain
As I lead my life
I ask you to not let me go astray…

Even though there are trials
And tribulations too
I pray that God guides me
And leads me all the way through…

Breakthrough of every obstacle
Breakthrough of every negative
Thought and deed
(Continued)

BREAKTHROUGH

Breakthrough of all the curses

That the enemy set up for me...

Breakthrough of poverty

Breakthrough in me

To keep a clean heart

So that I can remain free...

Breakthrough of all hurt

Breakthrough of doubt

Breakthrough of lies

That the enemy thought

Would take me out...

Well, devil

I am still standing

You thought you chose me

At random...

(Continued)

BREAKTHROUGH

Breakthrough
From the chains of abuse

Breakthrough
From the curses that were bestowed
Upon you.

Breakthrough to keep me in sane
Thank you God for placing
My feet in the right lane.
Breakthrough is what we all need
Regardless of the trial
God wants us to be free...

DON'T TAKE CONTROL OF MY MIND

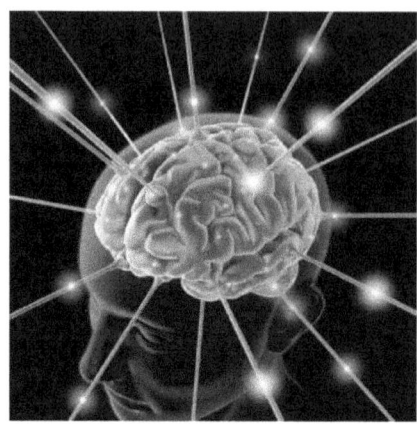

You can't take control of my mind
Because I won't let you
You can't take control of my mind
Because the love of God is true

You can't take control of my mind
Because I believe in Christ today
God is my savior
And has shown me the way

You can't take control of me
Because I have the power to succeed
You can't take control of me
Because God set me free

(Continued)

DON'T TAKE CONTROL OF MY MIND

You can't take control of me
Because God gave me a sound mind
You can't take control of me
Because the Word says, "Peace be Mine."

You can't take control

Of all I do
Because I am a believing the Savior
To work on me

You can't control me
Because I know who I am
I am a child of God
And he is my friend

You can't control
Because he loves me
You can't control me
Because I have the victory.

UNDERSTANDING WHO YOU ARE

Understanding Who You Are

Is very key in life

To understand who you

Is Unleashing God's purpose for your life.

Everyone has a purpose

Even though you maybe understand

What it may be

Seek God for your purpose

And pull it out of Thee…..

You are unique

You are a designer plan

You are an original

Like a blue print

That's exploding to stand…..

(Continued)

UNDERSTANDING WHO YOU ARE

You can stand alone

Without someone holding your hand

You have self-esteem

Without a woman or man...

For the purpose of God has been manifested

Not by work or deed

The purpose of God

Is that God believes in you and me...

Understanding who you are

Is key in life

Understanding who you are

Is not being defeated all through life...

We all have talents

And gifts within

Let's exercise what God

Has given us

And praise God for being a

A divine Friend.

Understanding Who You Are...

IF ALL EYES COULD SEE

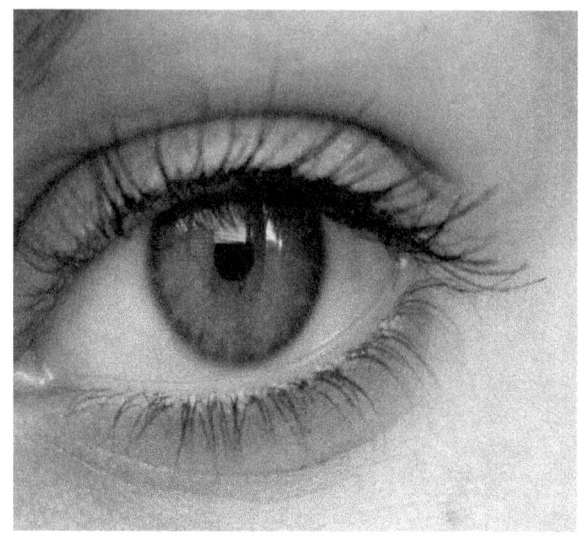

If all eyes could see
What God has done for me

If all eyes could see
The miracles he has
Worked out for me

If all eyes could see
I have the victory

If all eyes could see
The joy that I have in thine
(Continued)

IF ALL EYES COULD SEE

If all eyes could understand
That God is my man

If all eyes could see
I have hope

If all eyes could see
God loosened the ropes
The ropes of bondage

The ropes of pain
Now I have the glory
And can call His name

If all eyes could see
The past life I have lived
They would not judge me by
The color of my skin

If all eyes could see
They would love me
For who I am

(Continued)

IF ALL EYES COULD SEE

If all eyes could see

I am a true friend

If all eyes could see

I love deep within

If all eyes could see

I have anointing

If all eyes could see

I am appointed

KEEPING IT REAL

Yah, I am not perfect
Yah, girl that's me.

I am not perfect
I am sure the world
Can see

I am not perfect
That's why
I am still in the world
(Continued)

KEEPING IT REAL

I am not perfect

But I measure

To God's treasure

I am not perfect

So, don't judge me

Get your own

Soul right

So that you can be set free.

Keeping it Real

Is what I do

Keeping it Real

And fighting the devil too

Keeping it real

And knowing who I am

(Continued)

KEEPING IT REAL

Keeping it real

And taking a stand

Living life for what it is worth

Living each day

With a Godly approach

Keeping it real

Is what I do

Keeping it real

Even when I am blue

Keeping it real

Is being who you are

Keeping it real

And I still have sin

Keeping it real

So, Heaven will allow me in

THE EARTH HAS PURPOSE

We have been placed on the earth
With a divine purpose

We have been placed on this earth
For service

We have been placed on this earth
To witness to mankind

We have been placed on this earth
To love eternally

We have been placed on this earth
To help others see

We have been placed on this earth
To have victory

(Continued)

THE EARTH HAS PURPOSE

We have been placed on this earth
To seek God

We have been placed on this earth
To be meek

We have been placed on this earth
To understand faith

We have been placed on this earth
For God's sake

We have been placed on this earth
To keep it real

We have been placed on this earth
So the Holy Spirit
Can lead us day by day

We have been placed on this earth
For God to show us the way

We have been placed on this earth
To praise our way out

We have been placed on this earth

WHEN THE WAY HAS BEEN MADE

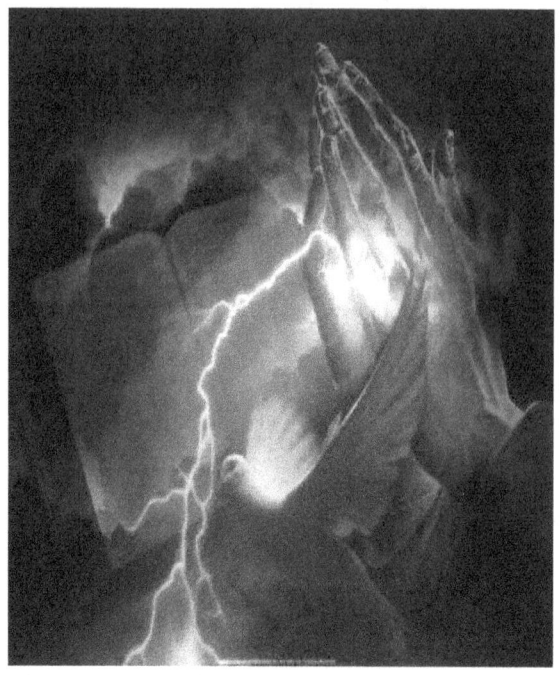

A way has been made
As God said, "It would be."
God wrapped his arms around me
And said baby you will be free…

Free from the judgments
That man has passed down
Free from the lies that
Took me down…

(Continued)

WHEN THE WAY HAS BEEN MADE

God said I forgive you

When the world holds you bond

I am the Lord

And my Word is what's sound…

You will no long be bond

By the cares of this life

Because I am the Husbandry

And You are my wife…

Look not to what man can give you

But look to me

I am your God

And have set you free.

FORGIVING

Forgiving can be difficult to do
God says forgive them
When we say we are through…

Forgiving means forgetting
And forgetting means forgiving
God says we must learn to love
If it's the last thing we do.
Help me, to love when I want to say, "Shew."
(Continued)

FORGIVING

The times that I have been told

That I can't achieve

Lord, hope me to forgive

And believe in Thee.

For you are my hope

You are my life

You are my love

You give me life…

You are my destiny

You are my dream

You are God

Thank you for forgiving and believing in me!

SHARING THE DREAM

The Dream lives within
The dream is me.
The Dream that we can live
In peace and harmony

The Dream of life
The dream of hope
The Dream that keeps us alive
The vision of God
That keeps us afloat.

(Continued)

SHARING THE DREAM

The dream of heaven
The dream of life
The dream that one day
We will have eternal life

The Dream of prosperity
One day it will be
The dream if spiritual abundance
Is the key

The Dream of Happiness
The Dream of Love
The Dream of Joy
The Dream and so it is,
The Dream that sets us free.

LOVING YOU IS EASY

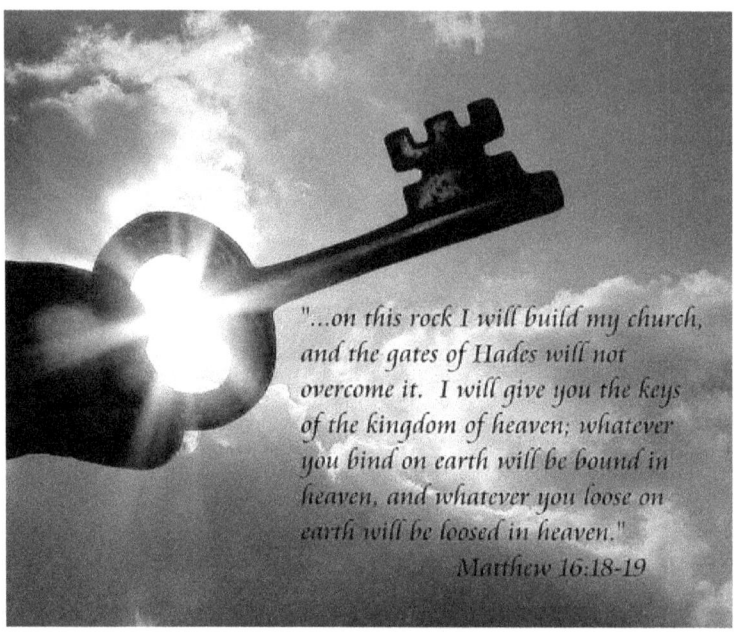

Loving you is easy

And so it appears to be.

Loving you is a dream

That one day will be.

Loving you is like a fantasy

That words cannot describe

Loving you is a dream

That I cannot deny.

(Continued)

LOVING YOU IS EASY

Loving God is easy
Because he created me
I love you Lord
Because you set me free.

Loving you is easy
Because in the midst of my storm
You hold my hands
And lead me on.

You believed in me
When I was down
You spoke to me until I
Came Around.

Loving you is beautiful
Can't you see
I love you, Lord
You set me free…

"Dedicated to Mother Nancy Russell, September 2009"
Spiritual Mother

LORD, I THANK YOU

Lord, I thank you
For Being a part
Of my life each day.

Lord, I thank you for
Loving me in every way.

Lord, I thank you
For giving me hope.

Lord, I thank you
For prosperity
Even when I felt
I am walking on a slope.

(Continued)

LORD, I THANK YOU

Lord. I thank you
For being my friend

Lord, I thank you
Because you are the man

Lord, I thank you
For who you are

Lord, I thank you
For being my superstar

Lord, I thank you
For providing for me

Lord, I thank you
For saving me

Lord, I thank you
For keeping me from death

Lord, I thank you
For being my true friend

UNDERSTANDING LIFE

Understanding Life is not
Always easy
Understanding Life is Not
What it always appears to be.

Understanding life can be
Difficult at times
Understanding life we can not explain
Sometimes.

(Continued)

UNDERSTANDING LIFE

Understanding life
You should give it to God
Understanding life is the love
Of your life

Understanding life
We can not comprehend
That's why God is
Your devoted friend.

ABOUT THE AUTHOR:

Alisha was born on August 1, 1969 at Beebe Hospital in Lewes, DE to the parents of Vaun Dyke Ford and Beverly Singletary. She was raised in Millsboro, DE and attended Indian River High School where she graduated in 1987. Alisha has two daughters Ashley and Amber Broughton. She attended Delaware Technical and Community College (1995) where she earned an Associates Degree in Early Childhood Education, later she attended Delaware State University (1987-1991) where she earned her BA degree in Journalism/English. In 2000 she earned her Masters degree in Special Education. Currently, Alisha is pursuing her Doctoral Degree from Argosy University in Washington, DC.

Alisha is a member of the National Association of Business Owners, The Delaware State Teacher's Education, The Maryland State Teacher's Association, The National Teacher's Association, The Milton Chamber of Commerce, The Milton Historical Society, Friends of the Milton Library, 2nd Vice President for the NAACP, a trainer subcontractor for the State of DE, Member of the Office of Minority Women, Owner and CEO of Unlimited Expectations Training and Consulting, LLC, Civic Association of Cool Spring, a volunteer and mentor the Delaware Breast Coalition, Delaware State University Alumni, Delaware Technical and Community College Alumni, Wilmington College University Alumni, Participant Purses for

Women Financial Literacy Program, Participant Score Program of DE, YWCA member, Editor for several books, Sunday School Teacher, Public School Educator, College Instructor, Sussex County Woman's Democratic Club, and 36th Democratic Party.

Alisha is currently employed by the State of DE and has been a teacher for several years. She is an instructor at Delaware Technical and Community College in Georgetown, DE and Delaware State University. She is writing her first book with hopes for publication in July 2009. She is a freelance writer for several Delaware Newspapers: Cape Gazette, Delaware State News, Coast Press, and the Sussex Post.

She has ten years of experience as group facilitator and trainer focusing on coaching and learning. She has been a host to a blog talk radio show. In 2006, Ms. Broughton was hostesses for a commercial, Vote or Die, Sean "Puffy" Combs also know as P. Diddy, for BET television. She currently provides coaching and seminars for personal and professional growth. She specializes in the design and implementation of trainings using team building tools. She has consulted and facilitated trainings for organizations within the U.S.A. She has taught her several college settings for 8 years and has been a public school teacher for 12 years.

Alisha attends Pilgrims Ministry of Deliverance in Georgetown, DE. She has served on multiple committees at her church. Alisha loves God and places Him first in her life. "God serves all the Glory in my life. He is the head of my life. He has brought me through miraculous experiences. He enabled me to raise my children as a single parent and has healed my body. God is good far beyond what I can ever express."

Letter from Apostle Ivory Hopkins and Pilgrims Ministry of Deliverance

God has graced Aisha Broughton with great insight and wisdom being a spiritual father to her and watching grow into a highly motivated and articulates woman of God it's a pleasure seeing her in print. Readers of her writing will be enlightened and helped by her years of experience.

A Proud Spiritual Father
Apostle Ivory L. Hopkins
Founder and Overseer of Pilgrims Ministry of Deliverance

Letter from the Members at New Zion AME Church

Congregation New Zion AME Church
Pastor Ouemonde Brangman and Sister Connie Brangman

Love you from your church family. We pray that God continuously blesses you!

Letter from Lakeia, Waneka and Vaun-Tae Broughton

Go Cousin, We love you! We are proud of you!

Letter from Vaun-Dyke Ford

I love you daughter! Keep up the awesome work. You are talented and that is no joke. You have exceptional skills that God has created in you. Your Father,

Letter from Delaware State University

Delaware State University

Wishes you success on your new book.

Class of 1990-1991 - Alumni

Congratulations

DSU Southern Campus

As an adjunct instructor

Wishes you success on your new book.

Class of 1990-1991- Alumni

Letter from Delaware Technical and Community College

Delaware Technical and Community College

Divorcing Parent

Corporate and Community

8 years as an adjunct instructor

Wishing you success!

Delaware Technical and Community College

Letter from Melodie Thomas-Price

A Leap of Faith Child Development Center

Lish, we have been friends for as long as I can remember. You are bad--girl. A diva for sure. I pray that God orders your steps. I love you and wish you much happiness and success in your life. This is just the beginning for you. Stay focused! God is going to take you places. I am here just ASK.

First Lady

Letter from Welton Evans

Thanks for being a business associate and friend. You are a special woman of God.

You are always willing to help others. I pray that your business Unlimited Expectations Training and Consulting, LLC, takes off like a rocket. You are an exceptional business woman. You are able to make anything work even when all odds are against you.

Letter from Beverly and Ben Singletary

Wow Daughter, In your 40 years you have accomplished much. We pray that God continuous to bless you! We pray that the favor of God falls on your life. We love you daughter--continue to walk in the authority that God has given you.

Mom and Dad

Letter from Ashley and Amber Broughton

Mom, we love you and are proud you. We guess we take the writing from you. We love to write as well. Because of you we are both in college and are striving to be successful professionals. We thank you for being hard on us and teaching us the way. Without you and God we do not know where we would be. For love you and thank you for being an exceptional single mom. You are special and we love you!

Letter from Mark Piper – MA Piper Trucking

(Written and Submitted before his passing in 2008)

I appreciate you for being there for me and helping me with my business. Girl, you can work miracles.

Letter from Mother Linda Lewis

I love you. You are an privilege to call a spiritual daughter and woman. Thanks for riding me places and having fun. You have an exceptional gift from God above.

Letter from Larcenia Metcalf

I love you and pray that God blesses you. You are an awesome diva, author, business owner, and evangelist. Thanks for helping me with the start up of my business. You are an awesome woman, mother, father, teacher, preacher and community activist.

Your Friend in the Gospel

Letter from Allene Broughton

I love you granddaughter you are the best. You are always there for me and I appreciate all that you do. I am glad that I have lived to see your success. I praise God that you have be blessed!

Keep serving God, Your Grandmother

PICTURES OF ME AND MY FAMILY

www.ingramcontent.com/pod-product-compliance
Lightning Source LLC
Chambersburg PA
CBHW071839290426
44109CB00017B/1867